FASHION DOGS

© 2002 Assouline Publishing for the present edition
601 West 26th Street, 18th floor
New York, NY 10001
USA
Tel.: 212 989-6810   Fax: 212 647-0005
www.assouline.com

First published by Editions Assouline, Paris, France.

Translated from the French by Bernard Wooding.
Copyedited by Margaret Burnham.

ISBN: 2 84323 340 2

Color separation: Gravor (Switzerland)
Printed in China

FASHION DOGS

BY FRANÇOIS BAUDOT

ASSOULINE

"The best thing about man is the dog."
Maxime du Camps

What other animal has been such a steadfast companion to man for thousands of years? What other animal has undergone so many transformations and fulfilled so many different functions? And what other animal has played such a big role in the well-being and lives of so many people? Fidelity, devotion, tenderness—no servant has ever served the interests of his master better. And none demands so little in return.

Our contemporaries, filled with a passion that is unique to them, lavish ever more attention on the dog, to the point of occasionally turning him into a full-fledged citizen. Leading leather goods manufacturers such as Hermès, for whom the making of leather leashes, harnesses and collars is an extension of its original vocation, today see the trendy dog as a new market, a clientele whose potential has yet to be explored. The elegant "O'Kelly" collar by Hermès ($260) has been followed by Paul Smith's designer leash, Gucci's sober little black coat, and Burberry's raincoat for dogs. Vuitton and Goyard also have specialized lines. Baskets, luxuriously padded rugs, cosmetics, organic dog biscuits and even mini one-room furnished apartments for homebody dogs all testify to the spread of His Canine Majesty's empire at the beginning of the third millennium. Things have gone so far that a "Palme Dog" was awarded at the 2001 Cannes Film Festival. Fashionable dogs even have their own websites, such as www.doggeneration.com financed by Royal Canin. Meanwhile, www.astrotoutou.com offers a horoscope for a species that, thanks to marketing, is clearly destined for a bright future.

This has been confirmed recently by the success in perfume stores of the spray *Oh My Dog!* In addition to this scent, intended for special outings, there is *Oh My Dog Is Fresh!*, a lighter eau de toilette intended for the humdrum routine of an everyday dog's life. The company estimates that in the space of a year some five hundred thousand dog owners have fallen for this scent, which some female dog owners have even confessed to using themselves, thereby reinforcing the fusion of beauty and the beast.

equally frivolous, but just as revealing, are the canine fashion shows now being organized. The New York magazine *Interview* recently devoted a whole issue to pets. It included a CD of music selected by Elton John to appeal to dogs' ears. It was also in New York, at Barney's, the trendiest of big stores, that cashmere dog pullovers were being snapped up for two hundred dollars apiece. Meanwhile, groomers, day-care centers and registered walkers are all making small fortunes.

Down the centuries, art has illustrated clearly the projection of human characteristics onto dogs. In addition to various minor painters who specialized in representing the dogs of high society, Andy Warhol, the leading light of Pop art, immortalized Moujik, Yves Saint Laurent's little bulldog, just as in the past Desportes, Oudry and Landseer represented the favorite dogs of aristocratic ladies or the finest greyhounds of the royal pack.

When the last dowager empress in China died in 1908, the head of the eunuchs, following a tradition dating back nine centuries, placed her favorite Pekingese at the head of the funeral procession. A griffon named Caesar, raised by the Duchess of Newcastle and presented to His Majesty King Edward VII by Lord Dudley in 1902, quickly became a heavy cross to bear for the whole of Buckingham Palace. During his master's funeral service, however, this griffon, who was not so much imperial as imperious, shed tears in front of the thousands of Londoners lining the route of the funeral procession. Walking with tiny steps between two horse guards, Caesar followed his master's coffin wearing a look of utter dejection.

The greyhounds that can be seen at the feet of the Duc de Berry in an illumination in the *Très Riches Heures* were used to taste the dishes at mealtime to ensure that nobody would be poisoned. Later, Louis XV was so fond of hunting that he used to feed his dogs personally in a sumptuous room adjoining the royal apartments. It was also said that after the execution of

Queen Marie-Antoinette, her faithful little Thisbée killed herself out of grief.

Conversely, the brutal death of Slipper, Wallis Simpson's cairn terrier who was cruelly bitten by a viper at the Château de Candy, caused his mistress such grief that her marriage to Edward VIII that same day was almost cancelled. The latter, who had become the Duke of Windsor following his abdication, ordered a charm for his wife from Cartier in the form of the slipper that the dear little departed dog loved to play with. Subsequently, the Windsors, a couple of eternal exiles, developed a passion for pugs. Each had its own silver bowl with its name engraved on it. And in the duchess's bedroom, bizarre cushions representing life-size effigies of the pampered dogs stood guard around the bed of this pathetic empress.

It would be incorrect to say that, historically, dogs were only owned by the great and good of this world. However, for a long time the pleasures of hunting were restricted to such people, and they were the only ones able to undertake the costly breeding of these carniverous companions. In addition, for numerous little princes who had to endure a solitary childhood, it was often the case that their sole confidant was a dog, the animal's inability to talk ensuring that they would never be betrayed.

rin Tin Tin, a four-legged star, was one of the few Hollywood actors not to be affected by the arrival of the talkies. Tintin's alter ego Milou, on the other hand, proved to be gifted at talking. And so, from the mastiffs painted by Velasquez to the weimaraners photographed by the artist

William Wegman, all representations of dogs in art, absolutely all of them, and to an even greater extent those featured in lifestyle images, exemplify the way the pooch, man's best friend, reflects man's passions, his silliness and his qualities. For between the dog and us, there remains only one link: a leash. One tugs at it and the other holds it, without either—man or animal—knowing who is really master of the other.

t hanks to wall paintings, we can date the domestication of the dog to around fifty thousand years ago. So why did this prehistoric animal decide to attach himself to the caveman? No doubt their interests complemented each other, starting with a shared taste for fresh meat.

Even today, the sight of a pack of hounds with their snouts buried in the entrails of a deer after they have been given the quarry, and the pleasure that such a spectacle evidently gives to so many hunters, takes us back to the dim and distant past, reminding us that both men and dogs are predators who live in very hierarchical clans.

Along the way, from one millennium to the next, man being the more intelligent of the two became leader of the pack, while the dog ate his leftovers. That is why dog follows man and obeys his gestures and words, for although dogs don't have very good sight, they have hypersensitive noses and discerning ears. "All that's missing is the ability to speak," it is often said when talking about a particularly expressive pooch. But isn't it the dog's very inability to speak, disagree or speak ill of someone that is so attractive and the reason for his unique status in the West?

"His largeness of size, his elegant form, the strength of his body, the freeness of his movements, all these external qualities are not the most noble things about this animal; and as we prefer the mind to appearance in man, courage to strength, emotions to beauty, we also feel that the inner qualities are what are most noble in animals; it is thanks to them that he differs from the automaton, that he rises above the vegetable, is close to us. It is emotion that ennobles his being, which governs it and vivifies it, which commands the organs, makes the limbs active, triggers desire and gives to matter gradual movement, will, life."

•

It would be hard to write a better homage to dogs than the above penned by Georges Buffon in his *Histoire naturelle*. He succeeds in tracing the frontier between the human and the animal, the conscious and the active, the complicity in the comparison. For while man is clearly seen by the dog as a sort of kindred spirit, be it dangerous or friendly, it is also not unusual for man himself to treat the dog like a fellow creature. This humanization takes the form of multiple projections, analogies and hunting metaphors, which would be amusing if they did not frequently reveal the mental chaos and the misguided confusion of the two, which a passion for animals can lead to.

One of the oldest pets, the dog occupies an intermediate place between cats, which have been treated as sacred or demonized, and the horse, which is much too large to live in the home. In Greek mythology, Cerberus, a three-headed mastiff, guarded the gates to hell, although the name was later used as a nickname for unpleasant concierges. Esculapius, Hermes and Diana the Huntress were also accompanied by dogs, as were Saint Hubert, Saint Eustache and Saint Roch. As for the recumbent statues in medieval churches, while the lord generally rests his feet on a lion, the symbol of courage, his wife generally has a modest greyhound at her side as the symbol of fidelity. As for the dog-lions that guard Japanese cemeteries, called *fochi* or "dogs of Buddha," although they are intended to look fearsome, they actually look more like irascible Pekingese rather than the king of the animal world.

however, the animal who has all too often become "granny's little doggy" knows how to become a dog of war or a guide dog for the blind when required, a police dog or performing dog, parade ground dog or guard dog. Neolithic, pre-Columbian or Chinese, the animal, from continent to continent, has served both the fur trade and scientific research. There is a dog constellation in the sky, and there was even a little pioneer dog in space at the end of the 1950s on board the Soviet Union's first *Sputnik*.

As for those who look like dog's dinners, underdogs, dog day afternoons, dog-eared books, the barking dogs that seldom bite, the dogs that have had their day, the sleeping dogs that are allowed to lie, the cats and dogs that fall from the sky, the old dogs you can't teach new tricks to, and the poor who are buried "like dogs," there are, from the top dog to the hot dog, a thousand metaphors that bear witness to the role of these remarkable creatures in society.

discussing dogs as a group seems enormously reductive, given the extraordinary diversification the animal has been subjected to and the varied uses to which he has been put during his historical and physical evolution. Dog's fur has been worn, his hide has been tanned, his flesh has been eaten. He has defended cities, delivered mail, tracked hares, hunted outlaws, flushed partridges, bitten the ankles of a thousand postmen, jumped into circles of fire, paraded in beauty contests, served as garbage collector, incarnated the perfect companion, powered wheels, saved children from drowning and climbers from certain death, and generated as many insults as he has performed helpful actions, from the Saint Bernard weighing around 70 lbs to certain Yorkshire terriers who are no wider than 3.5 inches.

Whether we praise him, lock him up, overfeed him, fear him, groom him, dress him up, beat him or shoot him (like a dog), he forgives us for everything. He lives through and for the masters to whom he has entrusted his fate.

Whether posing next to Charles V or following the tramp Charlie Chaplin, protecting Little Orphan Annie, listening to "his master's voice," guaranteeing the reliability of the Kléber tire or the humanity of the queen of England, from the Labrador to the pit bull you could rewrite the history of humankind through that of his four-legged companion. It could be said that the dog was the first instance of genetic manipulation. Indeed, this product manufactured out of the wolf or the dingo has never existed as such in the wild state. It requires all the ignorance of the city dweller to convince yourself that when you are with a dog you are in contact with nature.

At best, a dog is most natural when he urinates or copulates in public. In fact, the finest mongrels display sophistication, qualities and aptitudes that are well beyond most other animals. For tramps and jilted lovers, for loners and world leaders, a dog is often the ultimate companion, one whose pragmatism keeps you in touch with reality—the only one who can keep you from going nuts.

A Short Canine Glossary

Anthropomorphism. Man cannot resist endowing the dog with reactions and even emotions that could be those of his own conscience. This reciprocity has become a habit, but it remains paradoxical, especially if we remember that to be "treated like a dog" is generally pejorative.

Bichon frise and *se bichonner.* "Se bichonner" in French means to get dolled up, an action which is diametrically opposed to anthropomorphism. A woman who is grooming herself in front of the mirror is identifying herself with her little bichon frise dogs. A cross between the Maltese and the poodle, the bichon, with its short nose and its long silky coat, used to be very popular in France among ladies of little virtue—to the extent that, in an understandable confusion, they would sometimes say to a particularly generous customer: "See you soon, my little *bichon.*"

14

Biting. Aside from flight, a dog's teeth are its principal weapon. Whether playing or killing, whether in fear or by mistake, the dog bites the way a cat claws. There are many stories relating to bites from dogs and wolves, from the mysterious beast of Gévaudan in France to Pasteur's vaccination of a shepherd boy who had been bitten by a rabid dog.

Bone. The dog gnaws at it and can cut its teeth on it with complete impunity, because domestication requires his owner to provide for his basic need for food. Moreover, a beautiful bone that can be paraded proudly in one's jaws prior to burying makes a fine trophy.

Breed. In Europe, there are four hundred dog breeds, which were for the most part fixed between 1850 and 1930. They are divided into ten separate categories: sheepdogs are unique to each region; the guard dog attacks; terriers dig; dachshunds have short legs; spitz breeds are descended from sled dogs. Hounds, gun dogs and retrievers share the hunting tasks. As for companion dogs, they form the most numerous type today. That just leaves the aristocratic greyhound, which fulfills several of the above functions.

Breeding. Each dog breed is the result of rigorous selection and sometimes laborious mating. Most dogs find their owners through contacts made at clubs and competitions—paranormal meetings for adepts of the same sect. The remaining 42 percent are bought through commercial channels (as against just 14 percent for cats).

Flea. Inseparable from the dog, this jumping parasite is all the more fearsome in that it is practically invisible. Man only becomes aware of it when he sees his loyal companion wiggle. Scratching then becomes a big part in a dog's daily schedule. If the dog were to disappear, the flea would die of hunger.

"Here!" In its exclamatory form, the Latin *hic* is reserved almost exclusively for the dog. Generally followed by "Heel!," it is an order that demands immediate compliance, especially as it enables many owners to avenge themselves for the humiliations that they have to suffer in everyday life.

Kennel. In the 18th century, because toy breeds were susceptible to drafts, an elaborate range of indoor kennels, or doghouses, were created. By extension, "to be in the doghouse" is to be in a state of disfavor.

King Charles spaniel. This breed is firmly identified with a king, Charles II of England, who was crazy about these little dogs with bulging eyes. It seems only right that, after so many crowned heads had made so many different breeds of dog fashionable, that this one should now be particularly popular in modest households.

Leash. The leash binds man to dog and vice versa. In this mutual tugging, man has scored a decisive point with the invention of the retractable leash. By simply pressing the button on the handle, he can fix the little animal's field of action. Very popular in big cities, this rudimentary version of the remote control enables man to achieve one of his oldest dreams: instant obedience.

Nose. A veritable natural computer, the sharpness of its nose enables the dog to pick up, identify and decode thousands of smells, in places where man is only able to detect one or two. A dog's nose is its pride and joy. By extension, "having a nose" for something is a compliment when said about policemen as well as antiques dealers.

Role play. The dog resembles its owner, it is said, for no species so faithfully adopts the personality of its owner, who in turn ends up resembling his dog. The latter is so good at acting that he is often regarded as a ham actor.

Standing guard. Whether you leave a dog on its own in a car or at home, the most peaceable of dogs can turn savage at the approach of a stranger. "Cave canem" ("Beware of the dog")— as long ago as antiquity this inscription appeared on mosaics at the entrances to houses.

Stardom. From Rin Tin Tin to Rantanplan, the power of the dog in the media knows no bounds. The Hollywood exploits of the former held people of all ages in thrall, while the comical blunders and stupidity of the latter, Lucky Luke's comic book companion, have reduced successive generations to tears. Fine or foolish, however, the dog's rise to stardom has generally been a positive development.

Tail. The barometer that enables man to determine what mood his companion is in. A wagging tail is a good sign, but a tail between the legs is not so good. The severing of part or all of the tail according to the breed can be traced back to very old practices.

Television. Studies have shown that when a particular breed appears on television (generally for the purposes of advertising), it encourages people to acquire an equivalent specimen. Such fashions, alas, do not always outlast the momentary enthusiasm that prompted them—especially when the lovely fluffy animal turns out, after a few months, to be a hulking beast born to run five miles a day and to eat an appropriately large quantity of food.

WC. The street light remains the urban dog's finest conquest. He cocks his leg next to it with astonishing regularity. Apart from simply paying a call to nature, he is marking his territory. Wherever he goes he pees, before others, dragging their own blasé owners, come to sniff and then spray the post with three drops of acid of their own.

Xenophobia. A creature of habit, the dog tends to be hostile to anything unfamiliar. There are racist dogs, and there are those who are laid back. Sixty percent of bites are from German shepherds, three million of those nips going to the ankles of heroic postmen.

Zoophilia. "The more people I know, the more I love my dog." Love of animals knows no bounds, and this analogy can sometimes be taken to extraordinary lengths. Thus a mother sometimes appoints the family dachung to be her son's brother. Many owners consider their dogs to be full-fledged members of the family. For 20%, it's a child. Only 13% of owners see these our fine beasts as animals.

LANZUELA

BRVNETA

CLISANDRA COCVINA

BREDA ELVTVDO

ORLANDILLO

PIRAMO EL BLANCO FIDIELA

TIRLI

A

PERANETE

GRIS

DOGUE

woof a parody of the world's most famous fashion magazin

best bets for bow-wows!

the pick of the designer collections:
canine klein
yves saint bernard
ruff lauren

beau
bonus

grrreat grrroomin
an
magical makeove

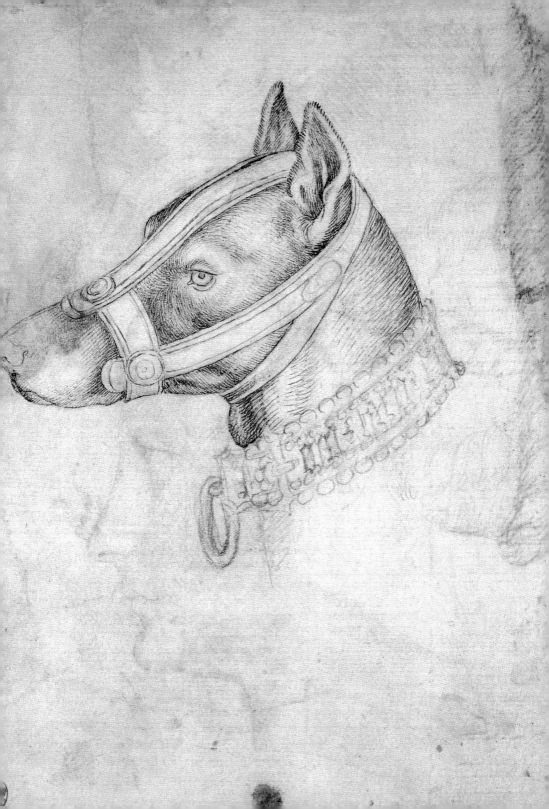

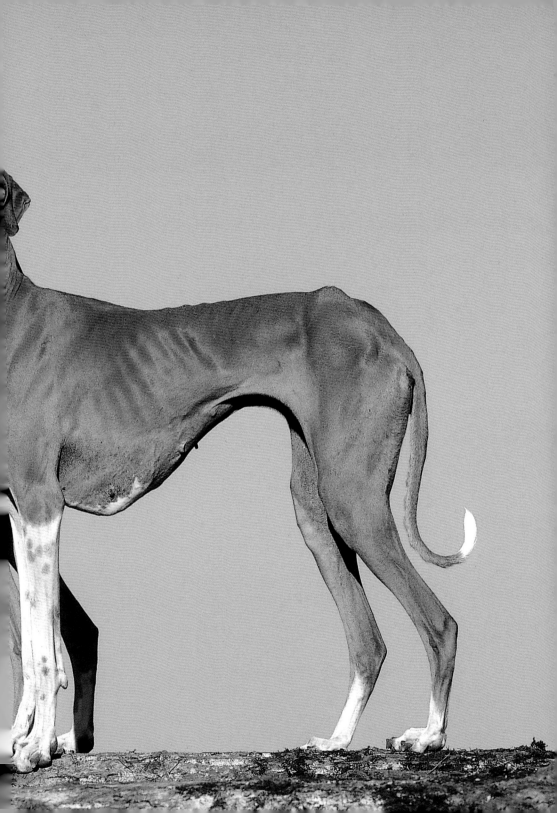

293

153

142

291

152

292

143

290

289

288

155

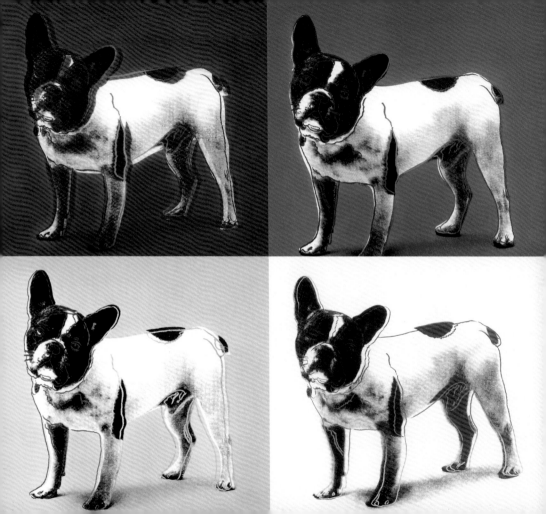

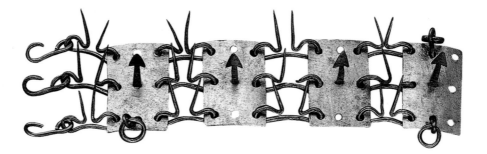

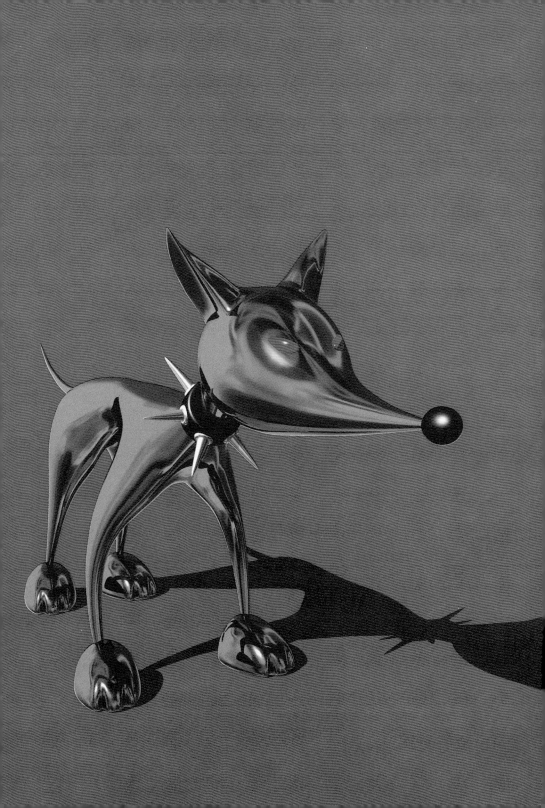

Nicknamed the "Dogaresse of Venice," Peggy Guggenheim, collector and patron, was here photographed on board her gondola surrounded by her loyal companions. Today they rest in peace near the tomb of this eccentric American. David Seymour, 1950. © Magnum.
After the perfume, the jewelry. Dog Generation launches the "Dog tag" for a "dog attitude." © Caroline Delmotte.

A dog's life in a château, against the backdrop of formal French gardens for these *Two Little Dogs,* an oil on canvas by Nicasius Bernaerts (1620–1678). Collections of the Musée du Louvre. © RMN/Arnaudet.

Colette in 1910. Dividing her time between writing and the music hall, the author of Claudine left some unforgettable pages on her search for equanimity through nature, the world of animals and, in particular, the dogs with which she used to surround herself. © Keystone.

The dog, the faithful companion of many politicians. Winston Churchill accompanied by the bulldog Barley Mow Token, on February 23, 1950. © Cecil Phillips/Keystone.
"New classicism" for Alfred Dunhill, by Keiichi Thara. Despite his powerful jaws and his intimidating growls, this English bulldog is a big softy. © Keiichi Tahara.

When you love, you do not count. *Lady with Dogs,* painting of the French school (16th–17th century), conserved at the Château de Fontainebleau. © RMN/ Gérard Blot.

Time for the daily walk. The duchess of Windsor and her pugs are surprised on the steps of the beautiful townhouse on the edge of the Bois de Boulogne where the Windsors lived. 1967. © All rights reserved.
Silver bowls that belonged to the duchess's dogs, stamped "F.B. Rogers Silver Company." © Sotheby's Archives.

In 1986, Ilène Hochberg launched *Dogue,* a parody of the American edition of *Vogue.* Fashion was by Yves Saint Bernard and Karl Dogerfeld, the jewels were by Bulldogari, the photos by Fido Scavullo and the "underwear" by Canine Klein. Photo Peter Serra. © D.R. **Head of a dog with a muzzle and collar,** by Pisanello (before 1395–1455). This preparatory drawing in pen and brown ink displays a sureness and rigor born out of direct observation. Musée du Louvre. © RMN/J. G. Berizzi.

Pair of Azawakh greyhounds. The greyhound was essentially used to chase hares. This beautiful, long-legged dog is fast and slender, the embodiment of the canine aristocracy. He often appears in medieval heraldry. © Labat/Cogis.

Before being crowned, Grace Kelly, future princess of Monaco, prepares her trunks under the mischievous gaze of her poodle. © Lisa Larsen/PPCM/Times Pix. **At the end of the 1920s, Hermès** were already producing luxurious catalogues in which man's best friend occupied an important place. © Archives Hermès.

Winner of a 1999 dog show, this shih tzu poses proudly next to his trophy. © Vedie/Cogis.
Dogs make bids too. This one was spotted during a jewelry auction in Geneva. © Photo Sacha Gusov/Christie's Images Ltd. 1999.

A fearsome weapon, this Doberman displays, in addition to his teeth, a studded collar that calls to mind the Hell's Angels' emblematic jacket. © Tony Garcia/Stone.
A particularly expressive Afghan greyhound. This dog has a remarkable coat which requires careful attention and inspired the hairstyles of numerous prominent people in the 1960s. © Labat/Cogis.

This *nishsiki-e* print from the empire of the rising sun shows a Japanese woman in crinoline walking her dog like a Westerner. *Woman and Her Dog*, 19th century. Musée des Arts Asiatiques-Guimet, Paris. © RMN/Thierry Ollivie.
Inseparable companions of country life, the horse and the dog. *Portrait of a Woman in Riding Habit with her Dog*, by Ferdinand Georg Waldmuller (1793–1865), Musée du Louvre. © RMN/Gérard Blot.

In a backyard in New York, in 1956, Alfred Eisenstaedt captured the writer Tennessee Williams walking his bulldog. © Alfred Eisenstaedt/PPCM/Times Pix.
Pug modeling a canine pullover design by Burberry in the company's famous plaid. © Burberry.

Joyce, a weimaraner (aged three), poses theatrically in its owner's salon in Passy. During the hunting season, she hunts during the weekend. © Kasia Wandycz.

The elegance of Gwyneth Paltrow in a sumptuous overcoat that matches the ebony black coat of her dog. © A. Southam/CPI/Cosmos.
On an armchair designed by Bertoia, the Chihuahua Peanuts presents a watch created by Chanel. © Jean-Luc Manson/Assouline.

On the Croisette in Cannes, Mutley, the president of the jury which in 2001 awarded a Palme Dog for the first time at the Cannes Film Festival. © Paul Cooper.
Like a lot of celebrities in the 1970s, the French bulldog Moujik, Yves Saint Laurent's favorite dog, posed for Andy Warhol, the prince of pop art. © Adagp, Paris, 2001.

Official portrait of Queen Elizabeth II with her corgi Spark, by Michael Leonard, 1986. © National Portrait Gallery, London.
Queen Elizabeth II's corgis receive special attention. She is rarely separated from them. Here, Her Majesty is carrying one of them in her arms after attending the Royal Windsor Horse Show. © Keystone.

The 101 Dalmatians, the famous Walt Disney cartoon of the 1960s, was inspired by this odd breed and launched a fashion that continued until the recent movie *The 102 Dalmatians,* in which Glenn Close, here with a funny Chinese crested dog, played the role of Cruella. © MPA-Stills/Foto Blitz.
Beauty and the Beast as seen by Helmut Newton in the 1980s. Raquel Welch with a large hound in Los Angeles. © Helmut Newton.

Publicity still for the first eau de toilette for dogs launched by Dog Generation. © Dog Generation.
Different types of dog collars (17th and 18th century). The steel spikes protected the necks of the dogs guarding the flocks from wolf bites. Private collections. © G. Symons. Collar with spikes (center) © Deutsches Jagd-und-Fischereimuseum, Munich/George Meister. Pictures taken from the book *Vie de chiens.*

"Doogy dogs." Left, Superlove sitting on his hind legs, or the power of seducing whoever you like and making them fall in love. As for Bad Doogy, right, he puts curses on people. © Dog Generation.

Mrs. Marjorie Post and her dog Scampi, whose canopy bed comes from the Belgian royal family, photographed by Alfred Eisenstaedt in the 1950s. © Alfred Eisenstaedt/PPCM/Times Pix.
Technological advances also impact on man's best friend. A bulldog presents a contemporary couch in brushed stainless steel with imitation leather cushions and shaved teddy, created for the webstore (www.le-webstore.com). © Thomas Esch.

An eagle-eyed recorder of Parisian life at the beginning of the 20th century, Jacques-Henri Lartigue here photographed himself accompanied by greyhounds. January 1926. © Ministère de la Culture-France/AJHL.
"A Dog's Life" in the third millennium as seen by Phong LD. © Phong LD/ Citizen K International.

A well-groomed, trendy dog, the poodle receives a lot of attention, in particular, grooming. © Hermeline/Cogis.
Close up of a Rhodesian ridgeback looking relaxed in his weekend outfit. © Getty images/Meredith Parmelee.

A Hollywood sex bomb of the 1950s, the curvaceous Jane Mansfield here poses with a poodle. Many men would happily have changed places with it. © Sunset Boulevard/Corbis Sygma.
A Chihuahua accessorized with a plastic flower and a precious collar. This breed, the smallest in the world, nonetheless produces some distinguished hunters in Mexico. © Liz & Jeff Van Hoene/Stone.

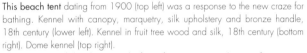

This beach tent dating from 1900 (top left) was a response to the new craze for bathing. Kennel with canopy, marquetry, silk upholstery and bronze handle, 18th century (lower left). Kennel in fruit tree wood and silk, 18th century (bottom right). Dome kennel (top right).
This dog seat (right-hand page) in the form of a miniature couch comes from Austria, early 19th century. © Musée et Jardins du Château de Vendeuvre, Calvados.

The bedroom of the Duchess of Windsor in Paris in the 1960s, with her collection of hand-painted velvet cushions representing her favorite dogs. Sotheby's Archives.
Young lady with her poodle, portrait by Birgid Allig. © Birgid Allig/Stone.

AIBO robot companion by Sony. It responds to its name with electronic barking, plays ball and reacts to stroking. A virtual personality that will delight its owners. © Sony.
The dog has always had pride of place at Hermès, as in this store window designed in 1998. © Guillaume de Laubier/Archives Hermès.

Louis Vuitton, like a number of other leather goods firms, has produced a few luxury accessories for fashionable dogs. This is a travel bag in monogrammed canvas. © Archives Louis Vuitton.
Jacqueline Bouvier in her teens, unaware that she would later become America's First Lady. Here she is pictured in East Hampton with a puppy at a time when she was known as Jackie. © Corbis Sygma.

The author and the publisher would like to thank Burberry, Dunhill, Hermès, Louis Vuitton, Philippe Couton (RMN), Claude D'Anthenaise (Musée de la Chasse et de la Nature), Matthew Bailey, Carole Bourriot (Magnum), Marie-Thérèse Canac, Françoise Carminati, Paul Cooper, Dog Generation, Dominique Deroche (Yves Saint Laurent), Sonia Elvira, Aude Fisch, Véronique Garrigues, Valérie Harel (Stone), Caroline Katgely (Sony), Luc Lemaire (*Citizen K*), Evelyne Leroix, Joanna Ling (Sotheby's), Gwendal Le Boulicaut, Joyce, Jean-Luc Manson, Valérie Merle, Mutley, Helmut Newton, Gwyneth Paltrow, Peanuts, Pascale Renambot (Cogis), Brigitte de Roquemaurel, Toby Rose, Catherine Seignouret (Keystone), Peter Serra, Keiichi Tahara, Barbara Tubaro, Madame de Vendeuvre, Kasia Wandycz, the webstore.